ILLUSTRATED BY ANDY ROWLAND

WRITTEN BY KATY LENNON

DESIGNED BY JOHN BIGWOOD AND JACK CLUCAS

STERLING CHILDREN'S BOOKS
New York

An Imprint of Sterling Publishing Co., Inc.
1166 Avenue of the Americas
New York, NY 10036

First published in Great Britain in 2019 by
Michael O'Mara Books Limited
9 Lion Yard, Tremadoc Road, London SW4 7NQ, England
© 2018, 2019 Buster Books

This book contains material previously published in *Colossal City Count*.

First Sterling edition published in 2019.
ISBN 978-1-4549-3403-5

Distributed in Canada by Sterling Publishing
c/o Canadian Manda Group, 664 Annette Street
Toronto, Ontario M6S 2C8, Canada

For information about custom editions, special sales, and premium and corporate purchases,
please contact Sterling Special Sales at 800-805-5489 or specialsales@sterlingpublishing.com.
Manufactured in China
Lot #:
2 4 6 8 10 9 7 5 3
08/19
sterlingpublishing.com

STERLING CHILDREN'S BOOKS
New York

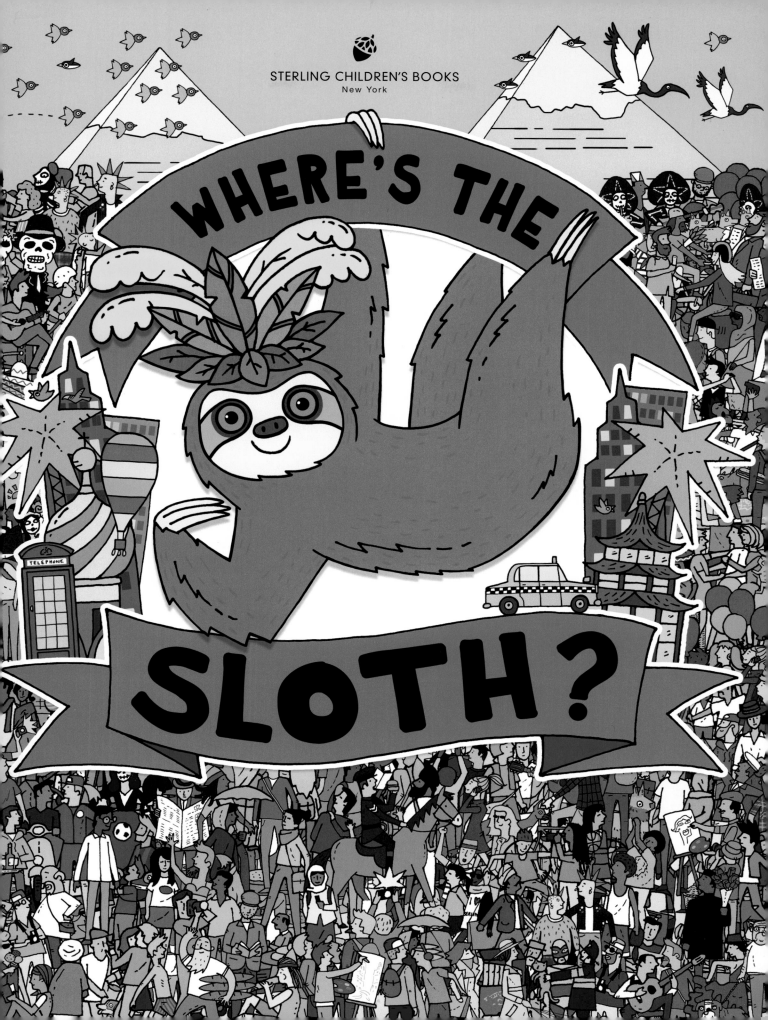

WHERE'S THE SLOTH?

INTRODUCTION

The sloths enjoy peaceful lives, hanging in the trees and relaxing away the hours. But ever since Suzi the sloth found a travel guide that was left in the jungle by a clumsy tourist, she can't help but wonder what's beyond the treeline …

Filled with a desire for adventure, Suzi has called on her sloth pals to join her on a round-the-world trip. Spot the 10 sloths in each of their new urban jungles and keep your eyes peeled for the other interesting items in the spotter's checklist at the back of the book. Bon voyage!

MEET THE SLOTHS

SUZI

Suzi has caught the travel bug. She has carefully planned a trip for her sloth pals so that they can explore as many different cities as possible.

BRADY

Brady is a sleepy sloth and struggles to do anything quickly. He's mostly looking forward to catching some ZZZs on the flight.

EMERALD

Emerald has a great relationship with the algae that grows on her fur. The green coloring that it gives her will really help her stand out in a crowd.

CAMILA

Camila likes to stay awake at night and is a real party animal. She can't wait to visit New York—she's heard it's the city that never sleeps.

JUAN

Juan is the oldest of the group. He's a history buff and is looking forward to visiting the ancient pyramids in Mexico and Egypt.

ANNA

Anna is very adventurous for a sloth and loves to swim. She can't wait to test the waters in Sydney and might even try surfing.

EVELYN

Evelyn is a baby and has much to learn about the jungle, let alone the rest of the world. Fortunately, she is a fearless sloth and wants to go sledding in Russia.

MANUEL

Manuel has a great party trick—he can turn his head almost all the way around. He loves yoga and is excited about visiting Delhi to practice with the yoga gurus.

INGRID

Ingrid is a big foodie who spends the days munching her way around the jungle. She's looking forward to branching out and trying some new tasty food.

ANDRÉ

André is ready to party and can't wait to visit the carnival capital of Brazil—Rio. He's even made a special headdress for the occasion.

TEOTIHUACÁN, MEXICO

The first stop on the sloths' grand tour is the ancient city of Teotihuacán [teh-oh-tee-wah-kahn]. It's bustling with tourists and taco sellers, and the sloths are impressed by all of the Day of the Dead skeleton costumes.

Juan is in his element and has rushed off to inspect the pyramids. Evelyn doesn't see what's so exciting about a pile of old bricks and is making friends with the local wildlife instead. Anna has been distracted by a rocking Mariachi band.

NEW YORK CITY, USA

The sloths have arrived in New York City, and it's hectic! They thought the birds in the jungle were loud, but that's nothing compared to the car horns and chatter of the city.

Camila is itching to find a party so she can dance the night away, while Suzi has a more civilized evening ahead and is going to see a Broadway show. Anna is hanging out in one of New York's famous cafés and having a delicious "slothee."

LONDON, UK

After a long flight, the sloths have touched down in rainy London. The city is buzzing with people going about their daily business and the sloths are struggling to keep up with the pace.

Manuel is looking forward to trying his first cup of English breakfast tea, and Ingrid is excited about travelling on public transit. Juan has spotted a bookstore and is going to hunt for his favorite novel, *The Call of the Wild*.

AMSTERDAM, NETHERLANDS

Suzi has brought the sloths to Amsterdam—the city that's known for its canals and clogs.

Manuel has hopped straight onto a bicycle and is touring the city on two wheels, with the wind in his fur. Being an art enthusiast, Suzi is off to create a masterpiece; she's hoping to be the next Vincent van Sloth. Ingrid is delighted by the tulips—she wonders if they will be as tasty as the hibiscus flowers that she's used to munching in the jungle.

GALERIE

BERLIN, GERMANY

The sloths are in Berlin and are starting to get used to all the tall buildings in the human world. They find the colorful graffiti that is dotted around the city particularly interesting.

Traveling is hungry work, so André makes a beeline for the bratwurst sausages. Emerald has spotted a group of punks and loves their spiky, multi-colored hair. She's hoping that they like her green fur—she's not sure if she would look good with a nose piercing, however.

PARIS, FRANCE

The sloths have developed a newfound love for cheese, and luckily there is plenty to sample in Paris—they can't brie-lieve it!

After a big cheese feast, Evelyn is trying to catch the attention of a nearby hot-air balloon pilot so she can ask for a ride and admire the city from above. Brady can't stop yawning and has found a sunny spot to curl up for a nap. Let's hope no one mistakes him for a living statue.

VENICE, ITALY

On the busy waterways of Venice, some of the sloths are enjoying being ferried around in long, elegant gondolas. Unfortunately, Emerald isn't used to water and waves—she's feeling a little seasick.

The first thing on the agenda for Suzi and Manuel is a tour of the city's beautiful churches and cathedrals. Evelyn and Anna have an excellent plan—they're heading straight for the first pizzeria they see for the biggest, cheesiest pizza they can find.

BARCELONA, SPAIN

The sloths feel at home in the laid-back city of Barcelona and plan to spend their time basking in the glorious sun. They're also going to visit the beautiful buildings that were designed by the architect Antoni Gaudí.

The colorful flamenco dancers have caught Brady's attention—he'd love to join in but can't move his feet fast enough. Ingrid is going to relax in a restaurant and eat a delicious seafood paella.

TIMBUKTU, MALI

In the West African city of Timbuktu, the sloth squad is in a busy marketplace. Everyone is friendly, but the sloths aren't sure about the strange humpbacked creatures—don't they know that spitting isn't polite?

Anna is searching the stalls for a new shirt to match her hat and is hoping to find a bargain. Ingrid is looking for some foodie inspiration and has found some delicious spices that she can't wait to experiment with when she gets back to the jungle.

CAIRO, EGYPT

The capital of Egypt is a fast-paced city with lots of people living in very close quarters. The sloths are getting used to the human world but think that it would do many people good to kick back, chill out, and be more sloth.

With the pyramids looming in the distance, Juan has gone in search of ancient Egyptian artifacts. Suzi is busy chatting with the friendly locals, and Evelyn is trying to avoid the huge, scuttling dung beetles.

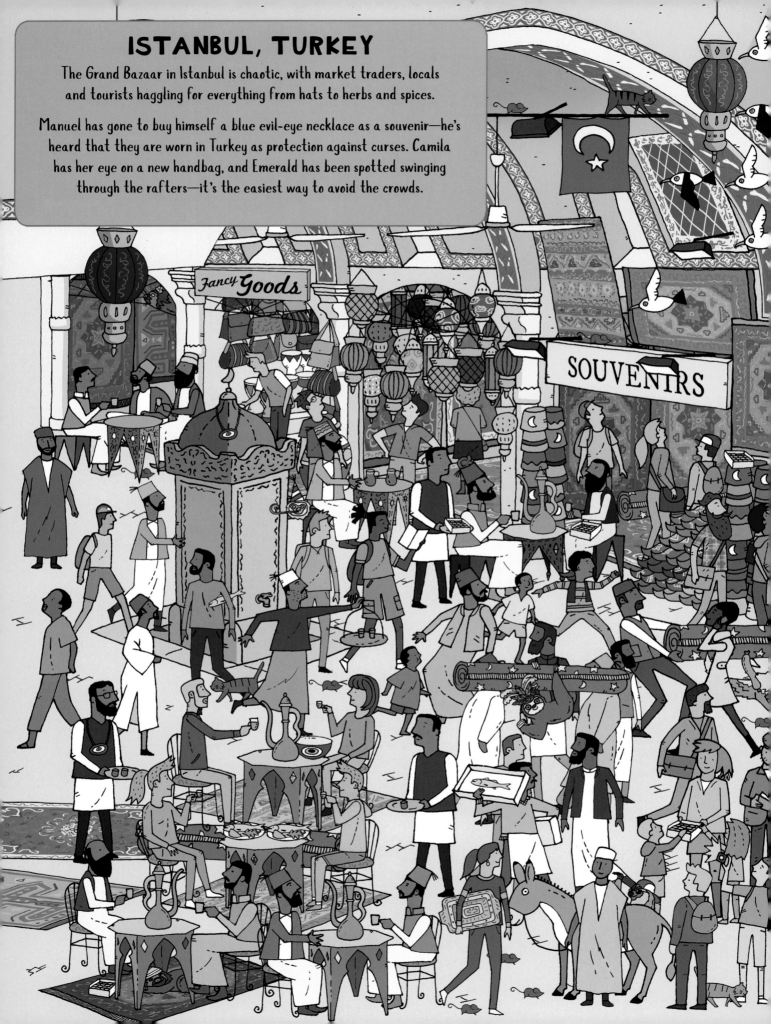

ISTANBUL, TURKEY

The Grand Bazaar in Istanbul is chaotic, with market traders, locals and tourists haggling for everything from hats to herbs and spices.

Manuel has gone to buy himself a blue evil-eye necklace as a souvenir—he's heard that they are worn in Turkey as protection against curses. Camila has her eye on a new handbag, and Emerald has been spotted swinging through the rafters—it's the easiest way to avoid the crowds.

Fancy Goods

SOUVENIRS

RUGS

SPICES

CERAMICS

SOUVENIRS

MOSCOW, RUSSIA

The temperature has plummeted in Moscow just in time for the sloths' visit. The gang have never seen this freezing-cold white stuff before (apparently it's called snow) and they really wish they had some thermal underwear.

The first to break away from the group is Evelyn, who has rushed off to join in with the sledding. Brady tried his claws at ice-skating but found it way too tiring. Juan feels like a cheeky kid again and is building a snow-sloth while pelting passersby with snowballs.

DELHI, INDIA

Back in a hot climate, the sloth pals are warming their fur in Delhi. Elephants, camels, bikes, and rickshaws fight for space on the roads, and the sloths quickly realize that they need to have their wits about them.

André has hailed a small car, called an auto-rickshaw, and is off on a tour of the city. Emerald, however, is more interested in traveling by camel. Manuel is practicing his balance before heading out of the city for a yoga retreat—he can't wait to show off his tree pose.

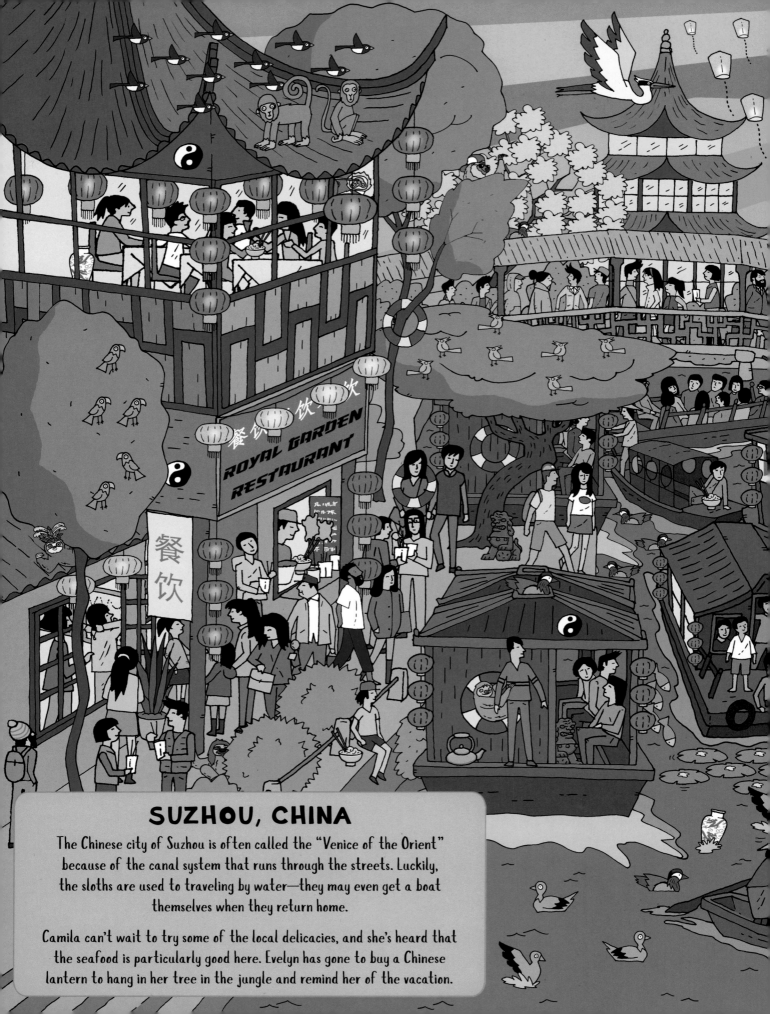

SUZHOU, CHINA

The Chinese city of Suzhou is often called the "Venice of the Orient" because of the canal system that runs through the streets. Luckily, the sloths are used to traveling by water—they may even get a boat themselves when they return home.

Camila can't wait to try some of the local delicacies, and she's heard that the seafood is particularly good here. Evelyn has gone to buy a Chinese lantern to hang in her tree in the jungle and remind her of the vacation.

TOKYO, JAPAN

Tokyo is a bright, neon jungle. The towering skyscrapers frame the mountains in the distance, and traditional culture mixes with the ultramodern in a unique and exciting way.

Emerald is on her way to see a sumo-wrestling match while Juan is going to sing his heart out in a karaoke club. Suzi has gone in search of the Tokyo Skytree, one of the city's most famous attractions. It must be a very impressive tree, but she's sure she's seen better in the jungle!

SYDNEY, AUSTRALIA

Sydney: the city of sun, sea, surf, and ... sloths! The laid-back Aussie attitude is just right for the gang who are all ready to kick back on the beach. All apart from Anna, that is.

Surfboard at the ready, she heads straight out to catch some waves—surf's up! Juan is slowly moving his way through the crowds to find a spot to do some "shade-bathing" and read his book. Ingrid doesn't want to get sand in her fur and is keeping watch with the lifeguards.

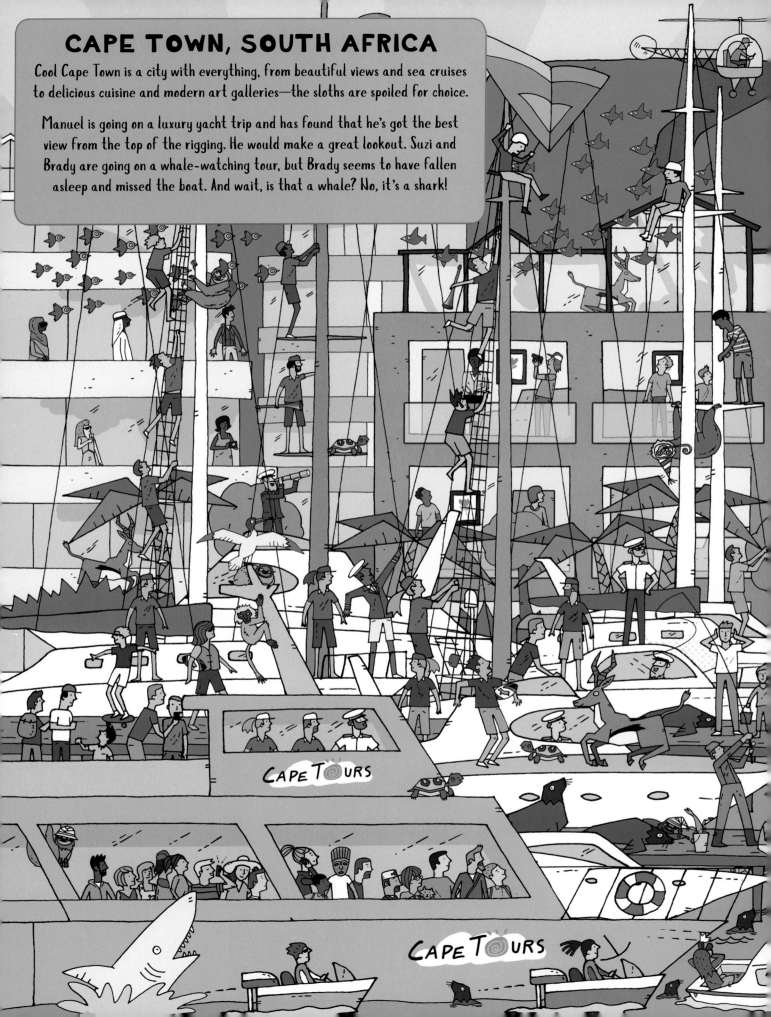

CAPE TOWN, SOUTH AFRICA

Cool Cape Town is a city with everything, from beautiful views and sea cruises to delicious cuisine and modern art galleries—the sloths are spoiled for choice.

Manuel is going on a luxury yacht trip and has found that he's got the best view from the top of the rigging. He would make a great lookout. Suzi and Brady are going on a whale-watching tour, but Brady seems to have fallen asleep and missed the boat. And wait, is that a whale? No, it's a shark!

RIO DE JANEIRO, BRAZIL

As the last stop on their adventure around the globe, the sloths are ready to let their fur down and party in Rio. Luckily it's carnival season and André fits right in with his stunning headdress.

Weaving their way through the spectators, Manuel and Anna find a place to sit and watch the parade. André wants to be in the thick of it and has climbed onto one of the floats. The crowds are going so wild, he feels like a carnival celebrity. What a way to end the vacation!

SPOTTER'S CHECKLIST

Two piñatas

Five donkeys

A wrestler in a purple mask and cape holding a balloon

A woman with a blue striped apron

Seven cacti

SPOTTER'S CHECKLIST

Three saxophones

A fireman saving a cat

Two policemen eating hamburgers

A person in a cowboy hat

Four racoons

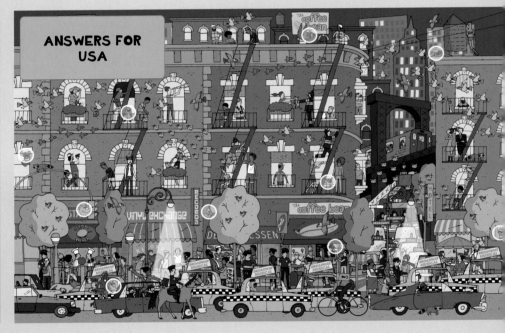

SPOTTER'S CHECKLIST

A pheasant

The queen and her corgis

A pigeon on a policeman's hat

Two Victoria sponge cakes

An orange cat

ANSWERS FOR NETHERLANDS

SPOTTER'S CHECKLIST

Five red bicycles ☐

Four wheels of Edam cheese ☐

Four paint palettes ☐

Someone falling into the canal ☐

A painting of a sunflower ☐

SPOTTER'S CHECKLIST

Three tubas ☐

Three guitar players ☐

A lady making giant bubbles ☐

A shop selling lederhosen ☐

A saxophone player ☐

ANSWERS FOR GERMANY

ANSWERS FOR FRANCE

SPOTTER'S CHECKLIST

Four watering cans ☐

An accordion player ☐

Four baguettes ☐

A high five ☐

Four Eiffel Tower ornaments ☐

ANSWERS FOR ITALY

SPOTTER'S CHECKLIST

A dropped ice cream

A proposal

Fish eating a pizza

A dog with a bow tie

A yellow umbrella

SPOTTER'S CHECKLIST

A person doing a handstand on a skateboard

Five bowls of paella

A baby in a highchair

A cleaner mopping the floor

An orange flamenco dress

ANSWERS FOR SPAIN

ANSWERS FOR MALI

SPOTTER'S CHECKLIST

Five ostriches

Three nuggets of gold

Two babies in slings

A well

A bucket on a string

ANSWERS FOR EGYPT

SPOTTER'S CHECKLIST

Four camels ☐

A pink-striped parasol ☐

Five Eye of Horus symbols ☐

A person with binoculars ☐

A horse and cart ☐

SPOTTER'S CHECKLIST

A donkey ☐

Four orange lanterns ☐

Six rolled-up Turkish rugs ☐

A dog stealing a sausage ☐

A green teapot ☐

ANSWERS FOR TURKEY

ANSWERS FOR RUSSIA

SPOTTER'S CHECKLIST

A collapsed snowman ☐

Someone throwing a snowball ☐

Four snowmobiles ☐

Four accordion players ☐

A set of matryoshka dolls (Russian stacking dolls) ☐

ANSWERS FOR INDIA

SPOTTER'S CHECKLIST

A cricket bat in a bucket

A tiger poster

Someone with a saucepan on their head

A game of cricket

Six peacocks

SPOTTER'S CHECKLIST

Five yin-yang symbols

Three blue-and-white vases

A giant turtle

A red handbag

A monkey with some noodles

ANSWERS FOR CHINA

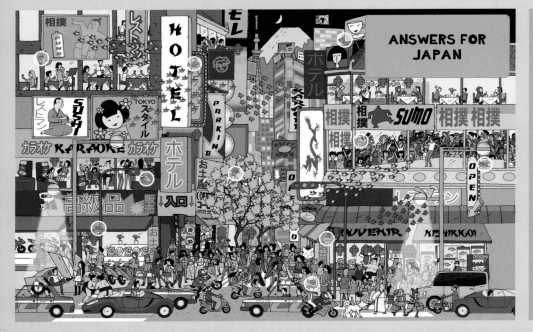

ANSWERS FOR JAPAN

SPOTTER'S CHECKLIST

Four sumo wrestlers

Three paper cranes

Five bonsai trees

A smiling teacup

A diner wearing a helmet

ANSWERS FOR
AUSTRALIA

SPOTTER'S CHECKLIST

A Christmas meal ☐

A koala on a man's leg ☐

A broken surfboard ☐

A lifeguard with binoculars ☐

A butterfly kite ☐

SPOTTER'S CHECKLIST

A cat on a boat ☐

A monkey wearing
a tribal mask ☐

An upside-down tortoise ☐

A fish being caught by
a fisherman ☐

A game of rugby ☐

ANSWERS FOR
SOUTH AFRICA

ANSWERS FOR
BRAZIL

SPOTTER'S CHECKLIST

A monkey with a soccer ball ☐

Three leopards ☐

Five red-and-blue frogs ☐

Four green lizards ☐

Five tarantulas ☐